# THE NO NONSENSE GUIDE TO BUYING AND SELLING OPTIONS

## LEARN WHEN AND WHY TO BUY OR SELL OPTIONS ON FUTURES CONTRACTS.

Michael K. Smith

ISBN-10: 1497305306
ISBN-13: 9781497305304

# FORWARD

This book contains no pictures, no charts, no graphs and most importantly no nonsense. It was written in an attempt to cut through all of the misinformation that so many option buyers and option sellers find so frustrating. You will not need a PhD. in mathematics or know the Greek alphabet to understand the contents of this book.

Most books on options paint unrealistic pictures of traders getting rich and they usually employ improbable cherry-picked examples of winning trades and trading strategies. Those books often avoid or minimize the fact that many option investors lose money. This book attempts to capture the reality of trading options on futures contracts from the perspective of a long time option trader and condense it down to its simplest form.

This book was written by a 20 plus year veteran of the futures and options markets who has made just about every mistake that there is when it comes to option trading. He has learned his lessons the hard way and hopefully you can learn from his mistakes. He is the founder of the futures and options brokerage company T& K Futures and Options, Inc. and is quoted frequently on various investment news media outlets such as *Bloomberg, Thompson Reuters, The Wall Street Journal, Market Watch* and *The Street.com.* He has worked one on one with futures and options traders from around the world.

For decades he has heard option sellers speak about how dim-witted it is to buy options when the odds are so disproportionately skewed in their favor. Then the option buyers retort that option sellers are dim-witted because they take unlimited risk positions for a finite and often very small profit potential. The fact of the matter is that both long and short options can be used depending upon the underlying market conditions. This book will attempt to show you when and why to choose to be either a seller or a buyer of options on futures contracts.

This book was written as a series of very succinct lessons and was kept short and simple on purpose. It is best suited for beginners and intermediate investors who have had some stock or commodity option trading experience in the past. It will also help hedgers to manage their future price risk using options. Hopefully, the brevity of this book will motivate you to read all of the lessons and develop your very own written trading plan.

# TABLE OF CONTENTS

# PART 1 THE BASICS

# LESSON #1 OPTIONS ARE VERY RISKY INVESTMENTS.

There is no such thing as a safe option investment. Option buyers are at risk for the entire premium paid plus commissions and fees. Option sellers have theoretically unlimited risk. Don't ever let anyone mislead you into thinking options are a low risk investment.

There are two types of options and they are calls and puts. A call option gives the holder the right but not the obligation to buy the underlying futures contract at a specific price (strike price) for a specific time period. A put option gives the holder the right but not the obligation to sell the underlying futures contract at a specific price for a specific time period.

As with all investments, option investors must manage their risk. The structure of a purchased option manages your risk to the finite level of zero but the odds are usually against option buyers. Option sellers must actively manage their theoretically unlimited risk but the odds are usually in their favor. Whether you are a buyer or a seller of options you must actively manage your risk to be successful.

## LESSON #2 VOLATILITY PREMIUM

It is this trader's opinion that the most important factor when deciding to be a buyer or seller of an option is implied volatility. The premium of an option is increased when the underlying asset's volatility increases. This is the point where most books would confuse you with ridiculous amounts of the Greek alphabet and complicated mathematical equations.

A simple way to guess how much volatility premium has been added to or subtracted from an option is by calculating the premium value. When this trader is deciding whether or not to buy or sell an option he will consider the costs of the options as a volatility premium indicator. Keep in mind some commodities have higher option costs most of the time. This occurs because some futures contracts are more valuable and more volatile than others most of the time.

Cost can be an excellent indicator for option investors as to when to be a buyer or seller of options. Your goal as an option trader is to find overvalued options to sell and undervalued options to buy. The idea is to learn to buy or sell options only when you have an advantage. If you cannot find trades that meet your buying and selling criteria you will not trade.

(When buying or selling options, this trader prefers to use a 4-6 month time horizon.)

Let's cover this trader's overly simplistic, often ridiculed approach to choosing potential options to buy or sell based entirely on price. If you can buy an at-the-money call or put option with 4-6 months of time until expiration for less than $1,500 this might be the time to consider buying that option. That's it.

Now let's apply this price based strategy to selling options. Your goal is to find an option to sell that is at least 25% out-of-the-money and has 4-6 months until expiration and is selling for at least $500 in premium. If the option meets these criteria, you may consider selling that option.

Let's be redundant to stress the importance of volatility premium. The logic behind the price based option buying and selling relates to the amount of volatility premium that has been added to or subtracted from the premium of the option. It is not often that volatility is high enough to enable you to sell an option that is 25% out-of-the-money with 4-6 months of time before expiration for $500. This forces you to trade only when option sellers have a clear advantage over option buyers. Conversely, it is only during periods of lower volatility that the markets will allow an option buyer to find 4-6 month, at-the-money options with a premium cost less than $1,500. Again this forces you to be disciplined and buy options only when you have a clear advantage over option sellers.

(We will cover later in this book a specific trading plan and checklist. Using a minimum and maximum option price is a component of that plan. You may want to modify these numbers based on your own goals, risk tolerance and trading abilities. The idea is to use option price as one specific element of your disciplined written trading plan.)

## LESSON #3 TIME DECAY

Options are wasting assets. Each and every day their premium is being eroded by time decay. Time decay is the best friend of the option seller and the worst enemy of the option buyer. As an option ages its premium is eroded more quickly and this is especially true during the last 60 days of an option's lifespan.

(This is one of the main reasons why option sellers often have an advantage over option buyers.)

## LESSON #4 INTRINSIC AND EXTRINSIC VALUE

The intrinsic value of an option refers to the amount an option is in-the-money. Let's use a hypothetical example to calculate the intrinsic value of an in-the-money crude oil call option. The premium value of the option is currently $3,125. The call option has a strike price of $100 and the underlying crude oil futures contract price is currently $100.45 per barrel. (The option is 45 cents in-the-money.) Crude oil is a 1,000 barrel contract and each one cent is equal to $10. The intrinsic value of the crude oil call option is $450. The rest of the option's premium ($2,675) consists of extrinsic value.

The extrinsic value of an option is made up of mainly time value and volatility premium. (Most investment glossaries disagree with this definition and define extrinsic value as being the same as time value. This trader does not understand why volatility premium is not mentioned in those definitions. Volatility premium plays a very critical role in the expansion and contraction of an option's premium. This is especially true when the options are out-of-the-money and their values consist of 100% extrinsic value.)

High demand for the specific strike price of an option can expand its premium as well. Quite often even numbered strike prices are more popular than odd numbered strike prices. In the crude oil example above the $100 strike price will most likely have more open interest than the $101 strike price and the $99 strike price.

## LESSON #5 CHOOSE MORE LIQUID OPTION MARKETS

My favorite markets are the Euro Currency, Japanese Yen, e mini Standard and Poor's Index, Treasury Bonds, WTI Crude Oil, Natural Gas, Corn, Soybeans, Wheat, Feeder Cattle, Live Cattle, Lean Hogs, Gold, Silver, Coffee and Sugar. These markets are liquid enough to trade effectively most of the time. This liquidity allows you trade in and out of your options easily and efficiently.

Sometimes Cotton, Cocoa, Copper, RBOB Unleaded Gas, ULSD Heating Oil and Orange Juice can be liquid enough to easily enter and exit with your option trades but the liquidity of these markets changes periodically. This liquidity increase can occur when a commodity market attracts the attention of large speculators such as hedge funds and large commodity trading advisors. Their buying and selling will increase the liquidity of the underlying futures market. This can often help to increase the liquidity in the options of the underlying futures contract.

Another variable that can increase the liquidity of normally illiquid markets is media attention. Sometimes the fundamentals of a particular commodity attract the media's attention which in turn can lead large and small speculators to those markets. This often adds more liquidity to those typically illiquid markets. It is during these times of increased attention and trading activity that the volumes and open interest in these markets can make them liquid enough to trade options effectively.

An example of a very illiquid market becoming relatively liquid during certain times of the year is the orange juice market. Weather events such as freezing temperatures or a potential hurricane affecting Florida can incentivize a much higher than normal number of option investors to speculate in orange juice option contracts. This increases the liquidity of those options and can make this frequently inefficient and dangerous market much more tradable.

Another example is the RBOB unleaded gas market. During most of the year this market has low volumes and open interest but during the spring and summer months speculators often begin to pile into unleaded gas options. They usually do this to try and take advantage of the "driving season" when most Americans get into their cars and travel to their vacation destinations. During the spring and summer months the options in the unleaded gas market regularly become much more liquid and efficient.

Usually, you do not want to get into a market with very low open interest and volume because quite often you will get taken advantage of by a large bid/ask spread when entering and exiting your option positions. This is often glaringly evident when buying and selling deep-out-of-the-money and deep-in-the-money options because there is often very little demand for those options.

Your goal is to be diversified between different sectors of the commodity markets and different markets within those various sectors. Make sure that the markets and strike prices that you want to invest in are liquid enough to trade.

(See the CONTRACT SPECIFICATIONS section at the end of the book to learn more.)

## LESSON #6 THE TREND IS YOUR FRIEND UNTIL IT ENDS.

You do not have to be a professional technical analyst to tell whether a trend is down, up or sideways. Stick with the trend. Most of this trader's counter trend option trades were losers. Picking the tops and bottoms of a market is a fool's errand. This trader recommends using weekly charts to see the trend for option trades. Weekly charts eliminate the hourly and daily "noise" in the markets allowing you to more easily uncover the macro trends that you are seeking.

## LESSON #7 POSITION TRADERS VERSUS DAY TRADERS

This book was written more from a position trader's mindset than that of a day trader's. There are pros and cons to both of these trading styles and you will have to decide which one fits your personality type the best.

A position trader is seeking a long term trend to follow. They are quite often much more interested in the long term supply and demand picture for the commodities that they trade than the short term charts and daily technical analysis. This type of trader will often stay in their trades for weeks and even months at a time. They are typically not as concerned with the day to day happenings in the underlying futures markets as a day trader might be.

A day trader on the other hand views the markets using a trading time horizon of seconds, minutes and hours. They will exit their "day" trades before the close of the markets on any given day. This means that they do not hold their trades overnight. These traders are usually very adept at technical analysis and use their technical indicators to facilitate their trading. Day traders quite often couldn't care less about the long term supply and demand picture for the commodities that they trade. They are usually only concerned about the daily market price trends.

## LESSON #8 FUNDAMENTAL, TECHNICAL AND SEASONAL ANALYSIS SHOULD ALL BE CONSIDERED BEFORE MAKING AN OPTION TRADE.

Fundamental Analysis

Supply and demand are the ultimate drivers of all commodity markets in the end. Over the near term hedge funds, large commodity trading advisors and large commercial traders can move the markets with their money but in the end supply and demand will dictate the price of a commodity. Therefore, you need to know the fundamentals of the market that you want to trade. There are many great resources on the internet for FREE. The United States Department of Agriculture and The Department of Energy are great resources and have weekly and monthly reports. A simple internet search can find you the association or government entity for just about any commodity out there. You can find a consolidated list of useful links for fundamental analysis at www.tkfutures.com/links.htm .

Technical Analysis

This trader uses weekly bar charts to find a macro trend in a specific commodity. Charts are very useful and will often mirror the underlying fundamentals of a market. Look for situations where the supply and demand picture matches the weekly charts. For example, when the supply and demand numbers are bearish for a particular commodity and the charts agree and are showing you a downtrend, look for bearish option strategies to implement.

Seasonal Analysis

Seasonal analysis is often misunderstood and mis-used. There are some very strong seasonal patterns that should be acknowledged when choosing an option trade. An example of a seasonal tendency that might warrant some credence is the tendency for soy-beans to find a bottom sometime in the September/October time frame as the U.S. harvest increases the supply of soybeans on the market. This does not hap-pen every year and weather and other factors will obviously affect this pattern but historical tendencies should be taken into consideration when looking for opportunities in options. There are a few companies that sell this information. An internet search of "sea-sonal futures patterns" will find you a list of compa-nies to choose from.

This trader recommends choosing trades in which the fundamentals are reflected correctly by the market's trend. If the seasonal trend does not match up it is not necessarily a deal breaker but it should certainly be taken into consideration. When the sea-sonal trend matches the fundamental and technical trends of a market, buying or selling options can be considered.

# LESSON #9 START WITH ENOUGH RISK CAPITAL.

**M**ake sure that you have enough risk capital before getting involved in option trading. This trader has seen too many underfunded option traders lose money. This probably occurs for a few different reasons.

1) Smaller accounts usually have to risk too much of their equity per trade. If they lose on their first trade or two it can take them out of the game before they get a chance to have a winning trade.

2) Smaller accounts are not able to properly diversify into multiple non-correlated markets. As with any type of investment, diversification is wise for option investors as well. It is very prudent to spread the trade risk between multiple markets to help minimize the exposure to a potentially losing trade.

3) Smaller accounts do not have the ability to control their position sizes and scale into and out of trades. This trader often recommends scaling into and out of your winning and losing trades. This is not possible if you do not have

enough funds in your account to enter into multiple option contracts at a time.

This does not mean that smaller accounts do not make money some of the time. However, being properly funded allows you to build a diversified option portfolio instead of "rolling the dice" on a trade or two. This trader believes that an investor planning on building a portfolio based on buying and selling options will need at least $50,000 to allow for proper diversification and the implementation of risk management procedures. This allows for diversification between multiple sectors of the futures markets and multiple markets within those sectors.

(Remember that selling options has similar risk to a futures contract and margin calls can and do occur. You will want to have plenty of cash cushion in your account when the inevitable short option trade "blow up" occurs.)

**NOTES**

**NOTES**

# PART 2 BUYING OPTIONS

# LESSON #1 LONG OPTION MECHANICS

The purchaser of an option is at risk for the premium paid (to the option seller) and the commissions and fees charged by the broker, exchanges and the National Futures Association. Purchased options are also called long options. The profit potential of a call option buyer is theoretically unlimited. The profit potential of a put option buyer is limited to whatever the difference is between the strike price and zero. This is because a commodity cannot be worth a negative number. It is absurd to think that an option trader will have a profit of infinity obviously;we are talking in theoretical terms.

(The person that sells an option buyer their long options has the other side of the trade and is considered to be short those options. Option sellers are also called option grantors or option writers.)

# LESSON #2 BUY AT-THE-MONEY OPTIONS IF POSSIBLE.

**A**fter years of trying complicated option buying strategies such as bull call spreads, bear put spreads, ratio spreads, straddles and strangles this trader now believes in the keep it simple method to choosing option strategies. These days the option buying strategy most often recommended by this trader is buying at-the-money call and put options.

At-the-money options are options whose strike price is exactly the same as the underlying future contract's price. Buying at-the-money options is not always feasible because the underlying futures contract is usually in motion. Let's assume that you have done your homework and decided that it is time to buy an at-the-money December corn call but when you are about to place the trade you see that the underlying futures price is at $4.04 ½ cents. Your choices of strike prices are the $4.00 and the $4.10.

(Your purchased option does not need to be exactly at-the-money. You can choose the $4.00 call that is 4 ½ cents in-the-money or the $4.10 strike price that is 5 ½ cents out-of-the-money.)

Example

For this example let's assume that the $4.00 call option costs $1,460 and the $4.10 call costs $1,225. This trader would most likely recommend the in-the-money strike price because it is still under the $1,500 maximum premium rule mentioned earlier.

(You could have also chosen the $4.10 strike price. One or two strike prices are not very important to the trading plan that will be outlined later but do not go more than three strike prices out-of-the-money when buying options.)

Advantages

The advantage to buying options is the limited risk profile and the profit potential.

Disadvantages

A long option can lose money a few different ways:

1) If the underlying futures market trades sideways the time decay will erode your premium and cause you to lose money.

2) If the market moves against you the option will lose money.

3) The market can also move in the direction that you expected it to and your option can still lose money. This can happen if the market does not move in your favor by enough to offset the commissions, fees, and time decay of your option.

4) A reduction in volatility can shrink the volatility premium within your option and can also cause you to lose money.

**NOTES**

# NOTES

# PART 3 SELLING OPTIONS

# LESSON# 1 RISK MANAGEMENT

Selling options on futures contracts has a similar risk profile to a long or short futures position. In the futures markets, traders often use stop orders to limit their losses. Option sellers can use stop orders as well or a mental stop if they are disciplined enough to do it that way. Many option sellers will cut losses (buy back) options that have doubled in value or begin scaling out of their positions as the market begins to move against them.

Example

Here is a hypothetical example of a natural gas option trade. You sold a $5.50 natural gas call for $500 and the option is now worth $1,000. You would buy back the option for $1,000 and take the $500 loss. This is much easier said than done because the markets do not always move in an orderly fashion.

(This trader recommends that you scale out of losing trades.)

Example

Let's use the natural gas example above to show you what it means to scale out of a losing trade. You are short 6 short natural gas calls and the premium has moved against you by 25%. You decide to buy back 3 of your options to limit your risk exposure. Let's assume again that your 3 remaining positions have moved against you by another 25%. You may decide to buy back another one of your options and so on and so forth.

(This is the decision of the trader and will of course have to be modified based on the risk tolerance of the individual. The idea is to have a written loss prevention plan in place before the actual trades are ever initiated.)

## LESSON# 2 DO NOT OVER LEVERAGE YOUR ACCOUNT.

This trader believes that using approximately 50% of your marginable equity is the maximum any option selling account should use. In other words, a $100,000 account should not use more than $50,000 of the available equity. The idea is to keep enough money in cash to avoid margin calls when the inevitable option trade mishap occurs in one of your short option trades. This money management technique can help keep you out of trouble.

## LESSON# 3 UNDERSTAND SPAN MARGIN

SPAN margin refers to the mathematical formula used by all U.S. exchanges to figure out what margin requirements investors need for short (sold) options. SPAN margin changes on a daily basis and is set by the exchanges. The SPAN margin requirement is approximately 150 to 200% of premium collected.

Let's look at a hypothetical example. You just sold a gold call option and collected $600 in premium and the SPAN margin requirement is $1,700. Take the total margin requirement of $1,700 and subtract the $600 of premium collected and this will equal $1,100. You will need to have at least $1,100 in cash to sell that gold call option.

(SPAN margin correlates closely to premium value of your option. If the option premium of the gold call that you sold in the above example increases by $200, then the chances are that your SPAN margin requirement increased by approximately $200 as well.)

## LESSON# 4 DO NOT USE MORE THAN 5% OF YOUR EQUITY ON ANY ONE TRADING IDEA.

Let's assume that you have $100,000 in your account and you want to sell November soybean calls for $700 each. Hypothetically, the SPAN margin requirement is $1,700 for each option. Take the total margin requirement of $1,700 and subtract the $700 premium collected and this will equal $1,000. This means that you can only sell 5 of those November soybean calls without going over 5% of your account equity.

(Obviously, if the market moves against you or the exchange raises its margin rates you will exceed your 5% equity level. Once the equity level reaches the 7-8% range, begin scaling out of your positions to get your equity level back below the 5% maximum. Margins rates are determined by market risk and the value of the underlying contract.)

## LESSON# 5 SPREAD OUT YOUR TRADES BETWEEN MULTIPLE NON-CORRELATED MARKETS.

If you choose from the recommended markets in the BASICS section of this book, it should not be hard to find 5-6 decent non-correlated trading opportunities at any given time. The key is to make sure that the markets you choose to trade are truly non-correlated to each other or at the very least exhibit a low correlation.

Some markets are very highly correlated to each other and should not be considered separate trading ideas. Crude oil, heating oil and unleaded gas are very highly correlated to each other. Heating oil and unleaded gas are distilled from crude oil and are therefore affected in a similar way by any price movements in crude oil. For instance, selling puts in crude oil, unleaded gas and heating oil should be considered one trading idea and your equity should be dispersed accordingly.

Soybeans and corn are often correlated because they are both feed substitutes for each other and they are planted in the same geographical regions which makes them susceptible to damaging weather events simultaneously.

Gold and silver are also correlated to each other at times. Both are considered precious metals and are often substitutes for each other when investors are seeking a hedge against inflation, currency risk, geopolitical risk, interest rate risk......

Quite often it is hard to find 10 different good trading opportunities. IT IS OKAY TO TRADE LESS. IT IS

OKAY TO USE LESS THAN 5% OF YOUR EQUITY ON ANY GIVEN TRADE. IT IS OKAY TO USE LESS THAN 50% OF YOUR TOTAL EQUITY.

If you decide to become an option seller you will be glad that you are not overleveraged on the day a lock limit move in the underlying futures contract of your short options is against you. If you trade options for long enough this will most likely occur at some point. Instead of ignoring this fact, you should plan ahead for it. That is why position size and diversification are so important when building an option portfolio.

(All U.S. dollar denominated commodities have an inverse correlation to the U.S. dollar which by definition means that they all correlate to each other to some extent. A strong U.S. dollar is often bearish for commodities in general because it makes it more expensive for foreign buyers to purchase U.S. commodities. On the other hand, a weak U.S. dollar is often bullish for commodities for the opposite reason. This is usually a loose correlation but this correlation does exist and should be taken into consideration.)

## LESSON# 6 YOU ONLY NEED TO LEARN 3 STRATEGIES TO SELL OPTIONS.

Credit Spreads

The credit spread is actually a limited risk trade. We will cover two types of credit spreads. They are the Bear Call Spread and the Bull Put Spread. Each of these credit spreads consist of a short option and a long option further out-of-the-money. The purchased option changes the risk profile from theoretically un-limited to one that is finite. This trader suggests using credit spreads only if the short option has 4-6 months until expiration and is at least 25% out-of-the-money and allows you to collect at least 10% of the total risk taken.

Example

Let's look at an example of a Bear Call Spread and let's also assume that the futures price of the underly-ing soybean contract is at $10 per bushel. You believe that soybean prices are going to go down.

Hypothetically, you sold a $12.50 soybean call (25% out-of-the-money) and collected $2,000. Then you bought a $14.50 soybean call and paid $1,000. Your end result is a premium credit of $1,000.

The risk profile of this trade is limited to the spread between the strike prices minus the premium collected. The contract size for soybean futures is 5,000 bushels and each one cent is equivalent to $50. There is a $2 difference between the two strike prices which is equal to $10,000. This leaves a total risk of $9,000 plus the commissions and fees that you paid. You collected approximately $1,000 and the risk is $9,000 which means your risk to premium collection ratio is above the 10% minimum.

Example

The bullish credit spread to use is the Bull Put Spread. This spread is the opposite of the Bear Call Spread outlined above. Let's use the hypothetical soybean example above. You would sell the $7.50 soybean put (25% out-of-the-money) and buy the $5.50 put.

(The premiums collected and the strike prices are somewhat ridiculous for these credit spread examples. It would require extreme volatility for you to be able to collect $2,000 for a soybean call or put that is 25% out-of-the-money. The strike prices on the Bull Put Spread are also unrealistic because soybeans may never see a price below $5.50 again. However, the example is meant to be overly simplistic and is useful because it outlines to you how these two credit spreads would be structured if you did decide to implement this strategy within your option trading portfolio.)

Advantages

There are a few advantages to credit spreads. They are limited risk trades and therefore are charged lower margin rates. They also allow you more staying power than a naked option strategy because the purchased option offsets some of the losses that will accrue if the market moves against you. Remember, as the soybean market rallies higher, your purchased call in the Bear Call Spread is accruing in value while the short call is losing money and vice versa for the Bull Put Spread.

Disadvantages

The main drawback to a credit spread is the time horizon for holding onto this trade. You will usually have to hold credit spreads longer than the other naked option selling strategies that we will cover to optimize profits.

(Naked option sellers often buy back the options that they sold to lock in profits before expiration. Credit spread traders often stay in the trade until expiration day or they exit a few days before when there is very little time value left in the option premium. To fully maximize credit spreads, short strangles and selling naked calls and puts you would have to hold the options until expiration.)

Risk management strategies for credit spreads are similar to the naked option strategies. You will cut your losses if the position moves against you causing your premium collected to double or you will scale out of your spreads.

Short Strangles

A short strangle is often used in markets trading in a well defined price range. It consists of selling an out-of-the-money call and an out-of-the-money put. This trader suggests using this strategy only if you can sell options with 4-6 months until expiration that are at least 25% out-of-the-money and allow you to collect at least $500.

Example

Let's use the crude oil market for this hypothetical example. The underlying crude oil futures contract is at $100 and you sold a $125 call option and a $75 put option. The call option collected $700 and the put option collected $500.

(It is often the case that call premiums are higher than put premiums because there is typically a higher demand for call options.)

Advantages

The advantages to short strangles include lower margin rates and offsetting price movements. Because you are playing both sides of the market, the exchanges often view a strangle as a more conservative trade than selling naked options on one side of the market or the other. This strategy can work well in sideways trending markets.

Short strangles can also offset each other as the underlying market moves up or down. Let's assume that you entered into the crude oil strangle above and the market begins to rally higher. Obviously, this is bad for the call option that you sold but the put option will help to offset some of those losses because it is gaining as the call option is losing.

Disadvantages

The main drawback of the short strangle is the vulnerability of an increase in volatility of the underlying futures contract. A rapid increase in volatility will most likely increase the volatility premium on both the call and the put that you sold and both sides of the trade can move against you.

You might also have a huge price breakout on one side or the other. This might quickly double the premium received and your risk management strategies must be implemented as quickly as possible.

Use the doubling of premium risk management strategy to limit any losses in short strangles or the scaling out procedures. In the example above, $700 was collected on the short call. Cut your losses if the premium reaches the $1,400 level for that option or begin scaling out of the position. The short put collected $500. Cut your losses if the premium reaches the $1,000 level or begin scaling out of the positions for every 25% that they move against you.

Naked Calls and Puts

Selling naked calls and puts brings chills to the spines of many option traders. Selling a naked call when you are bearish a market or selling a naked put when you are bullish a market is the simplest option selling strategy that exists. This trader suggests using this strategy only if you can sell options with 4-6 months until expiration that are at least 25% out-of-the-money and allow you to collect $500.

Advantages

The main advantage to this strategy is its simplicity. This strategy can be used in markets with a defined up or down trend.

Disadvantages

The main drawback is the risk profile. At any time the underlying futures contract can sustain a huge price breakout against your positions. The unlimited risk profile of this trade should again be managed by incorporating the doubling of premium or the scaling out procedures mentioned before.

**NOTES**

**NOTES**

# PART 4 DEVELOP A WRITTEN

# TRADING PLAN

# LESSON #1 CREATE A PERSONAL WRITTEN TRADING PLAN.

It is this trader's belief that a personal written trading plan is the most crucial component of an option trader's tool box. Each trader should develop their own written trading plan that will be followed at all times. Quite often the single biggest inhibitor of an option trader is themselves. These markets are very adept at exposing one's character deficiencies and a written trading plan helps traders stay disciplined during the tough times.

So many option traders lack the ability to detach emotionally from the markets and their trades. They lack discipline and often hold their losers way too long and exit their winners way too early. Their egos and pride can often cloud their judgment to the point of paralysis. Soon the trader has arrived at the point when wishes, hopes and faith become part of their trading plan. This in turn quite often leads to those portfolio killing trades that can negate months and years of profits in a period of hours and days.

Many traders will develop a very well thought out and practical trading plan for choosing and entering their trades but they never give any thoughts to exit strategies. DEVELOP A WRITTEN TRADING PLAN COMPLETE WITH ENTRY AND EXIT STRATEGIES FOR BOTH WINNING AND LOSING TRADES.

## LESSON# 2 CREATE A CHECKLIST FOR YOUR WRITTEN TRADING PLAN.

**E**ach individual trader must develop their own written trading plan based on their unique risk tolerances and abilities. This is much easier said than done but it is <u>absolutely</u> necessary. Use the trading checklist example below to help you create your own option trading checklist.

**Option Trading Checklist**
1) Check the technicals.
2) Check the fundamentals.

3) Check the seasonals.
4) Find a contract 4-6 months out.
5) Check option prices.
6) Choose your option strategy.
7) Devise an entry strategy.
8) Devise an exit strategy for losses and profits.
9) Confirm that your trading ideas are non-correlated.
10) Place your trades.

Let's go through a hypothetical example of the thought processes you might use to choose your various option trades using your written trading plan and trading checklist.

Example
You just opened a self directed trading account and deposited $100,000. You have been using a "demo" account version of the trading platform that your brokerage offers for the last two weeks. You are now comfortable enough to go "live" with your trades and use the "live" trading platform.

(Demo accounts will be covered in more detail in the FIND A GOOD BROKERAGE FIRM section later in the book.)

# TRADE #1

1) You look through the weekly charts of the commodities that you follow and you see a downtrend beginning in the sugar market. (Bearish)

2) You do your fundamental analysis and find that there is a global surplus of sugar and demand is currently falling. (Bearish)

3) You check your seasonal chart for sugar and find out that sugar often sells off this time of year coinciding with the sugar cane harvest in Brazil. (Bearish)

4) You check the available contract months for sugar and find the July contract has 150 days left until expiration. (This fits nicely into your 4-6 month option time horizon.)

5) You check the call option strike price 25% out-of-the-money and it is only selling for $112. (This does not meet your $500 minimum for selling options rule.) You then check the at-the-money put strike price and the premium is $950. (This does meet your less than $1,500 at-the-money option buying rule.)

6) You decide that the best option strategy for this particular instance is purchasing at-the-money puts.

7) You decide that you really like this trade and you will go all in. Because you are a disciplined option trader, all in to you means up to 5% of your equity. You decide to buy 5 of the at-the-money July sugar puts for a total cost of $4,750 plus commissions and fees. (This meets the 5% or less of your equity rule for a trading idea.)

8) You decide that your loss strategy will be to exit all 5 of your put options if the premium goes down by 50%. You decide that your exit strategy for profits will be a gradual scaling out of the positions for each 25% increment that the options accrue in value. (3 at 25%, 1 at 50% and 1 at 75%)

9) This is your first trade so there is no need to decide if it is non-correlated to your other trading ideas.

10) You open your trading platform and place your very first option trades.

Are you ready to look for another trade?

# TRADE #2

1) While you were checking the charts of your favorite commodity list you noticed that natural gas has been trading in a well defined sideways pattern with approximately a $2.00 price range. (Sideways trend)

2) Your fundamental analysis comes up with the recent Energy Information Administration report from last Thursday that showed the underground supplies of natural gas are right in the middle of their 5 year average. The demand numbers are very average as well. (Sideways trend)

3) The seasonal chart on natural gas shows a tendency for natural gas to rally at this time of year. (Bullish) You check the price charts and see that natural gas is near the top of its recent trading range but is now beginning to sell off. (Bearish-You decide that these two contradictory bullish seasonal and bearish technical trends offset each other and fit into the sideways trend idea that you are trying to take advantage of.)

4) You check the available contract months for natural gas and find a contact with 132 days until

expiration. (This fits into your 4-6 months option time horizon.)

5) You check the call options for natural gas 25% out-of-the-money and they are selling for $700. (This fits your $500 minimum for selling options. You check the put options 25% out-of-the-money and they are selling for $500. This also fits your $500 minimum for selling options.)

6) You decide that the best strategy for this particular instance is a short strangle. You check the margin requirements and after the premiums are collected they will total $900 per strangle.

7) You like the trade but you remember how volatile natural gas can be so you decide to enter into only 3 short strangles in the April natural gas market. The initial margin requirement is $2,700 plus your commissions and fees. (This meets the less than 5% of your equity rule.)

8) You decide that your loss exit strategy will be to scale out of one option at a time if they move against you by 25% increments. Your profit exit strategy is to simply let the options expire worthless.

(You realize that there is a chance that one side of this strangle may move against you while the other side profits. This is why your loss exit strategy is based on each individual option and not each individual strangle.)

9) Sugar prices do not correlate to natural gas prices. (Non-correlation confirmed)

10) It's time to place your trades.

## TRADE #3

1) As you continue to peruse the weekly charts of the commodities that you follow you notice that crude oil seems to have bottomed and is now trending higher. (Bullish)

2) You check the weekly crude oil energy reports and discover that crude oil supplies are very low as compared to their 5 year average and the demand season for unleaded gas is coming soon. (Bullish)

3) You check your seasonal charts and discover that crude oil often bottoms around this time of the year. (Bullish)

4) You check for available contract months and find a contract with 149 days until expiration. (This fits into your 4-6 month option time horizon.)

5) You check the at-the-money call options and the premium is $2,450. (This does not meet

your less than $1,500 at-the-money option buying rule.) You check the put options 25% out-of-the-money and find that they are selling for $630. (This is above your $500 minimum rule for selling options.)

6) You decide that the best option strategy for this particular instance is a naked put. You check the margin requirements and they are $1,450 per naked put after the premiums are collected.

7) You decide to sell 3 naked May crude oil puts. The initial margin on this trade is $4,350. (This meets the less than 5% of your equity rule.)

8) You decide that your loss exit strategy will be to scale out of one option at a time if they move against you by 25% increments. Your profit exit strategy will be to let the options expire worthless.

9) Crude oil prices typically do not correlate to natural gas and sugar. (Non-correlation confirmed)

10) It's time to place your trades.

# TRADE #4

1) You check the charts again and find a potential trend change in the July soybean contract. Soybeans seem to have made a bottom in February and are now trending higher. (Bullish)

2) You check the most recent United States Department of Agriculture supply and demand reports and find that the carry over stock piles are low and the stocks-to-usage ratio is also very tight. Chinese demand for U.S. soybeans has been robust and is expected to continue. (Bullish)

3) You check the seasonal chart for soybeans and find that often soybeans do take a "February break" and rally afterwards. (Bullish)

4) The July soybean options have 131 days until expiration. (This fits into your 4-6 month time horizon.)

5) You check the at-the-money call options and they have a premium of $1,480. (This meets your less than $1,500 at-the-money option buying rule.)

6) You decide the best option strategy is to buy July soybean at-the-money calls.

7) You decide to buy 3 July soybean calls for $4,440 plus commission and fees. (This meets the less than 5% of your equity rule.)

8) You decide that your loss exit strategy will be to cut losses on all 3 options if they move against you by 50%. You decide that your profit exit strategy will be to scale out of your positions one at a time for each 25% increase in premium.

9) Soybean prices do not correlate to sugar, crude oil or natural gas. (Non-correlation confirmed)

10) It's time to place the trades for your account.

**NOTES**

## NOTES

# PART 5 HEDGING WITH OPTIONS

# LESSON #1 HEDGING 101

So far this book has focused on using options for speculation purposes only. However, options are quite often used for hedging purposes. Producers and consumers of commodities often use options to protect themselves from future price risk. Derivatives of exchange traded futures contracts "options" did not come into existence in the United States until the late 1970s but the history of hedging using exchange traded futures contracts began more than a century earlier.

In the middle part of the 1800s the first futures exchanges in the United States were created. These futures exchanges were the Chicago Board of Trade (est. 1848) and the New York Cotton Exchange (est. 1870). These exchanges facilitated price discovery and price stability for corn and cotton buyers and sellers. This helped both the producers and the consumers of those two commodities hedge their price risks more effectively. Before long many other agricultural futures contracts were created to meet the growing demand for these hedging mechanisms.

To fully appreciate the importance of hedging one can envision the United States in the 1800's as an agrarian based society dependent upon farming for its survival. During harvest times there was typically such an abundance of a commodity versus the demand that the farmer may be forced to sell his crops for little or no profit. Conversely, during planting times there was often a lower supply of a commodity versus the demand and the farmer could charge exorbitant prices. These potentially large price swings could affect both the producers and the consumers of a commodity adversely.

The advent of the futures markets allowed commodity producers to lock in a selling price for their crops before they were harvested. This enabled them to more efficiently budget their money for input costs such as seeds, fertilizer, bank loan interest payments, storage and distribution. The consumers of the commodity also benefitted from the futures markets by having the ability to lock in the price that they were willing to pay before the crops were planted. The ability to hedge their future price risk and the relative price stability that the futures markets created helped both the consumers and the producers of a commodity.

## LESSON #2 HEDGING WITH OPTIONS VERSUS FUTURES

**H**edging with options does have advantages over hedging with futures contracts. Hedging with a futures contract locks in a forward price for the specific commodity. If the commodity being hedged moves to a more favorable price level after the hedge is initiated the hedger cannot capitalize on that favorable price movement because he has already locked in his price level with his futures contracts. Using options to hedge is more like buying an insurance policy. It protects the hedger if the market moves adversely against them but it also allows the hedger to reap the benefits of a favorable move in the underlying commodity being hedged.

Hedging with futures contracts also involves posting margin. Margin is a good faith deposit that must be posted to the account before the futures trades can be initiated. If the underlying futures market moves against the hedge, the hedger may be required to add more margin money to the account to hold onto the futures contracts. Futures contracts have a theoretically unlimited risk profile. On the other hand, the purchaser of an option contract has paid in full up front and there is no risk of a margin call. This means that the option hedger knows in advance the entire cost of the option hedge and entire risk exposure as well.

Example

Let's look at an example of how a corn farmer who expects to have 5,000 bushels of corn to sell can set a price floor for his corn using at-the-money put options. The formula for establishing a price floor is (strike price) plus (basis forecast) minus (premium paid for the put). Let's say that the December corn futures price is $5.00 and the put option strike price is $5.00 as well. Let's also assume that the expected basis is .06 cents and that the premium cost of the put option is .30 cents.

(Basis is the difference between the cash price and the futures price of the commodity.)

The price floor formula for the hypothetical example above would be $5.00 plus .06 cents minus

.30 cents = $4.76. The price floor for the corn farmer would be set at $4.76 per bushel.

Now let's imagine that 4 months have passed since the hedge was initiated and it is November 21st which is the expiration date for the December put option. It is time for the farmer to sell his physical corn. The futures price of December corn is now at $4.40 per bushel and the cash price is $4.46 per bushel. (Futures price plus the .06 cents basis)

The intrinsic value of the $5.00 corn put would be .60 cents. ($5.00 strike price minus $4.40 current futures price = .60 cents)

The farmer paid .30 cents in premium for the option. This cost will be subtracted from the intrinsic value. (.60 cents intrinsic value minus .30 cents premium cost = .30 cents)

Add these .30 cents to the current cash price of $4.46 and the farmer's price floor of $4.76 still holds true. He successfully hedged his price risk to receive a minimum of $4.76 for his 5,000 bushels of corn. He can now sell his physical corn and exit his option hedge and collect $4.76 per bushel for his corn.

# LESSON #3 OPTIONS CAN BE USED TO HEDGE YOUR STOCK PORTFOLIO.

**M**any savvy investors use options to hedge the risk in their stock portfolios. Long put options can be used as a hedge against potential stock market declines. Let's assume that you want to hedge your stock portfolio from an expected decline. Below is a hypothetical example of your effort to hedge a portion of your stock portfolio.

Let's say that you were lucky enough to enjoy a 25% return in your stock portfolio last year. It is now January and you believe a 10% correction is imminent over the next 6 months. For this hypothetical example let's also assume that the Standard and Poor's Index (S&P) is at 1750. A 10% correction would send the market down to the 1575 level.

For this example of a stock portfolio hedge we will use the e mini S&P option contracts. The contract specifications for the e mini S&P are $50 multiplied by the index. Each one point is worth $50. Let's assume that each put option costs $2,900. (As a hedger you are using options as a method of buying insurance for portfolio protection and not speculating. Therefore the less than $1,500 premium rule for purchasing options does not apply.)

Example

You decide to buy 5 June 1750 e mini S&P puts for a total cost of $14,500. Your goal is to offset some of your potential losses in your stock portfolio if you are right about the coming stock market correction. You calculate that your put options will be worth $43,750 if the Standard and Poor's Index sells off to the 1575 level before the expiration of your June put options.

Let's review the math.

1750 minus a 10% correction = 1575

1750 minus 1575 = 175 points

175 points multiplied by $50 = $8,750 per option contract

5 put options multiplied by $8,750 = $43,750

(This would be your intrinsic value of your options at expiration if the underlying futures market is at 1575. If the 1575 level is reached before expiration there will be extrinsic value added into the option premium as well.)

The portfolio hedging strategy in the hypothetical example above had a total cost of $14,500. If you are wrong and the correction does not come within the 6 month time horizon you will lose the $14,500 that you invested. (This potential loss example assumes that you do not cut losses and hold onto the options until expiration.)However, if you are correct your e mini S & P put hedge will help offset your portfolio losses by $29,250.

## LESSON #4 OPTIONS CAN BE USED TO HEDGE COMMODITY PRICES.

M any knowledgeable producers and consumers of commodities hedge their price risk by using call and put options. A producer of a commodity such as a farmer, rancher, oil driller, gold miner etc. is most worried about the prices for the commodities that they produce going down. They can buy put options to protect themselves.

The consumers of those commodities such as a food processing plant, a refinery, a jeweler etc. are most worried about prices going higher. They can buy call options to protect themselves against adverse price movements. Options can be used as a form of price risk insurance for both producers and consumers of commodities.

Let's look at a hypothetical example of a corn farmer trying to hedge the price risk of his upcoming crop. For this example let's assume that December corn futures prices are at $5.50 per bushel and that it is the end of May and he has just finished planting his available acreage. This farmer expects to harvest 100,000 bushels of corn this year. Each contract of corn leverages 5,000 bushels and each one cent per bushel move equals $50. The farmer remembers the $3.00 per bushel decline that happened a few years ago and he is worried that corn can go as low as $4.50 per bushel this year.

Example

He decides to buy 10 December corn $5.50 put options to protect a portion of his expected harvest. The total cost of these options is $14,000. If the December corn contract goes down to the $4.50 level he calculates that his corn puts will be worth $50,000.

Let's review the math.

$5.50 minus $4.50 = $1 (100 cents)

100 multiplied by $50 = $5,000 per put option contract

$5,000 multiplied by 10 contracts = $50,000

(This would be the intrinsic value of the farmer's options at expiration if the underlying corn futures contract is at $4.50 per bushel. If the $4.50 price level is reached before expiration there will be extrinsic value added to the option premiums as well.)

The producer hedge in the hypothetical example above would cost the farmer a total of $14,000. If he is wrong and the $1.00 correction does not occur by the expiration of the December corn puts he will lose a total of $14,000. (This potential loss example assumes that the farmer does not cut his losses at some point.) However, if he is correct his corn put hedge will help to offset the losses of his physical corn by $36,000.

Let's look at a hypothetical example of a consumer hedge. This example features a jewelry fabricator who will need to purchase 1000 ounces of gold over the next 90 days and is worried about an increase in gold prices. The gold market has been very volatile lately and he wants to protect himself from a potential $100 per ounce price move to the upside that he believes may occur. Gold is a 100 ounce contract and each one dollar move per ounce equals $100. The current price of the June gold futures contract is $1,250 per ounce.

Example

The jeweler decides to purchase 10 June gold $1,250 call options for a total cost of $23,000. He calculates that if gold prices rally by $100 per ounce over the next 90 days his call options will be worth $100,000.

Let's review the math.

$1,350 minus $1,250 = $100 per ounce

$100 multiplied by $100 = $10,000 per call option contract

$10,000 multiplied by 10 contracts = $100,000

(This would be the intrinsic value of the jeweler's call options at expiration if the underlying gold futures contract is at $1,350 per ounce. If the $1,350 level is reached before expiration there will be extrinsic value added to the option premiums as well.)

The consumer hedge in the hypothetical example above would cost the jeweler $23,000. If he is wrong and the $100 move in gold does not occur by the expiration of the June gold calls he will lose a total of $23,000. (This potential loss example assumes that the jeweler does not cut his losses at some point.) However, if he is right his gold call hedge will help to offset the losses in his physical gold purchase by $77,000.

**NOTES**

# NOTES

# PART 6 FIND A GOOD BROKERAGE FIRM.

# LESSON #1 FIND A BROKER WHO KNOWS HOW TO SERVICE YOUR SPECIFIC TRADING NEEDS.

Self Directed Traders

This trader has found that most self directed traders are not fully autonomous and need help every now and again. This is especially true when they first start using the trading platform. If this is the category that you fit into then you will want to not only find a fair commission rate and a good trading platform but also a seasoned broker to talk to if you have a problem or concern. You will usually have to pay a couple of dollars more for the services of a veteran broker but they can be extremely valuable if you make a trading mistake and need their help. Make sure to find out if you can have a broker who is dedicated to your account so you can speak to the same person every time you have a question or concern. A good broker can act as a second pair of eyes for your account.

A good broker may also:
- Call you to make sure that you did not forget the GTC order in your account even though you just offset all of your open positions in that market;
- Check your account every morning to make sure there were not any trading errors from the previous day's trades;
- Call you when you are getting close to a margin call;
- Call you to ask why all of a sudden you are trading soybeans instead of the e mini S&Ps that have been the only market that you have traded for the last few years; Did you hit the S instead of ES or is the account number wrong on the trade?
- Alert you to the fact that it is First Notice Day so you don't have to take delivery of a box car full of wheat;
- Enter and exit a trade for you if your computer crashes……..

Most trading platforms are similar in the attributes they offer but some have higher monthly platform fees than others. Make sure to find out what platform costs are involved before opening your account. Higher platforms fees do not necessarily indicate that a trading platform is better than a trading platform with lower fees. There are some professional grade trading platforms that are very inexpensive so shop around before opening an account with a brokerage that charges high platform fees.

Many commodity brokerages offer a free practice demo account for you to use for at least two weeks. These demo accounts are usually funded with $50,000 of phony virtual equity. This enables you to practice your trading and get familiar with the markets and the trading platform with no real financial consequences. Typically, these demo accounts will give you limited real time quotes but most quotes will be delayed by 15-20 minutes. Make sure that the brokerage company that you choose offers a free demo account for their trading platform. It is very important for you to be comfortable with your trading platform before going "live" with your trading. An errant click on buy instead of sell or on 100 contracts instead of 10 contracts can be a very expensive trading mistake.

Broker Assisted Traders

A broker assisted account is for traders who want to be hands on with their trading but lack the time, knowledge or inclination to trade their own accounts. Your broker will suggest trades and risk management strategies based on your individual risk tolerances and comfort levels.

These accounts are non-discretionary which means the broker will not do any trades at their own discretion and therefore they must approve each trade with you before placing them. If this is the type of trader that you are then you will want to find a broker who has at least 5-10 years of actual trading experience and understands both selling and buying options.

(Very few brokers are comfortable doing both within the same portfolio so make sure to ask them what their favorite option trading strategies are for buying and selling options on futures contracts. Some brokerage firms do not allow their brokers to suggest option selling strategies because of the potential margin call issues that can occur.)

The broker will be qualifying you by asking you questions about your investment experience, risk tolerance and available risk capital so make sure to ask him your list of questions too. It is a two way interview in which each of you is deciding whether or not to do business with the other. Make sure to ask the broker if they have a written trading plan for their broker assisted clients. If they do not have a written trading plan call another brokerage until you find one that does.

# NOTES

**NOTES**

# PART 7 RISK REITERATIONS

# LESSON #1 ALWAYS EXPECT THE UNEXPECTED.

Risk has been covered time and time again throughout this book because it is so important to manage your risk exposure when trading options. The futures markets are truly a 24 hour global marketplace and can be affected by events anywhere in the world at any time. A terrorist attack or a natural disaster on the other side of the world can turn your profits into losses while you are sleeping. It is very important for you to stay up to date with your markets.

You must look at option trading from a risk management perspective and actively manage the risk in your portfolio on a daily and trade by trade basis. This does not mean that you will have to be glued to your computer screen all day to effectively manage your option portfolio. It does mean that you should check your trades at least once or twice a day. In this age of hyper connectivity in which smart phones are ubiquitous there are not too many times during the day when the normal option trader is totally unplugged from technology.

This trader has tested his connectivity from the top of the Rocky Mountains in Colorado and from the middle of Everglades National Park on a flats boat and was still able to use his cell phone. The point is that there are very few cellular dead spots in the United States anymore. These days there is no reason not to check up on your trades at least once daily. Staying in tune with the markets is one more way for you to manage your portfolio risks.

(Risk and profit potential are proportional to each other. In other words, for you to make above average profits you will by definition have to take above average risks.)

# CONCLUSION

The original goal of this book was to create a truthful and useful book to help option traders become more successful. It is the author's sincerest hope that this book has added some clarity for you regarding the real world of buying and selling options on futures contracts. It would be a great compliment if you find this book useful enough to use it as a desk reference and apply its lessons as a guideline to create your very own written trading plan.

*If the harsh realities and the risk disclosures contained within this book did not scare you away from buying and selling options, then turn the page and you will find even more options on futures educational resources for **FREE**.

For more **FREE** educational resources visit www.tkfutures.com

Visit this website and you will find:
- Charts and quotes
- Contract specifications
- Current margin rates
- Trading hours
- Option contract mechanics
- Futures contract mechanics
- Futures and option trading strategies
- Detailed information on your favorite commodity markets
- Free Practice Demo Accounts
- Links to various government and private fundamental news resources
- And much, much more…….

**NOTES**

# NOTES

# GLOSSARY OF TERMS

**At-the-money option-** An option with a strike price that is equal to the current market price of the underlying futures contract.

**Ask-** The price at which a party is willing to sell. Also referred to as the "offer".

**Backwardation-** A futures market in which the distant contract months are higher in price than the nearby month.

**Basis-** The difference between the current cash price and the futures price of the same commodity. Unless otherwise specified, the price of the nearby futures contract month is generally used to calculate the basis.

**Bar Chart-** A chart that graphs the high, low and settlement prices for a specific trading session over a given period of time.

**Bear Market**- A period of declining prices.

**Bid**- An expression indicating a desire to buy a commodity at a given price, opposite of ask.

**Broker**- A company or individual that executes futures and options orders on behalf of financial and commercial institution and the general public.

**Bull Market**- A period of rising prices.

**Call Option**- An option that gives the purchaser the right but not the obligation to purchase (go long) the underlying futures contract at the strike price on or before the expiration date.

**Carrying Charge**- For physical commodities such as grains and metals, the cost of storage space, insurance, and finance charges incurred by holding a physical commodity. In interest rate futures markets, it refers to the differential between the yield on a cash instrument and the cost of funds necessary to buy the instrument. This is also referred to as the cost of carry or just carry.

**Closing Price**- The last price paid for a commodity on any trading day.

**CME Group**- Chicago based exchange that is the world's largest futures and options exchange. It was formed in 2007 through a merger between the Chicago Mercantile Exchange and the Chicago Board of Trade.

**Commercial**- Term used to describe futures traders whose primary business is in the underlying physical commodity markets.

**Commodity Futures Trading Commission**- A federal regulatory agency established under the Commodity Futures Trading Commission Act of 1974 that oversees futures trading in the United States.

**Consensus**- (Often called "bullish consensus") The perceived opinion-either bullish or bearish-of traders in a specific market. If a substantial majority of the market is perceived to be bullish, this may be an indication that the market is overbought and should therefore be sold. The opposite is true if a substantial majority is perceived to be bearish.

**Consumer Price Index (CPI)**- A major inflation measure computed by the United States Department of Commerce that measures the change in prices of a fixed market basket of 385 goods and services of the previous month.

**Contract Month**- A specific month in which delivery may take place under the terms of a futures contract.

**Cost of Carry (or Carry)**- For physical commodities such as grains and metals, the cost of storage space, insurance, and finance charges incurred by holding a physical commodity. In interest rate futures markets, it refers to the differential between the yield on a cash instrument and the cost of funds necessary to buy the instrument.

**Crop Reports**- Reports compiled by the United States Department of Agriculture released throughout the year covering planted acres, yield, and expected production. It also supplies a comparison of production from previous years.

**Customer Margin**- Within the futures industry, there are financial guarantees required of both buyers and sellers of futures contracts and sellers of options contracts to ensure contract obligations are fulfilled. FCMs are responsible for overseeing customer margin accounts. Margins are determined on the basis of market risk and contract value. This is also referred to as performance bond margin.

**Daily Trading Limit**- The maximum price range set by the exchanges for a futures contract.

**Day Traders**- Traders who take positions in futures and options and exit them before the close of that trading day.

**Deliverable Grades**- The standard grades of commodities or instruments listed in the rules of the exchanges that must be met when delivering cash commodities against futures contracts. Grades are often accompanied by a schedule of discounts and premiums allowable for delivery of commodities of lesser or greater quality than the standard called for by the exchange.

**Delivery**- The transfer of the cash commodity from the seller of a futures contract to the buyer of a futures contract. Each futures exchange has specific procedures for delivery of a cash commodity. Some futures contracts, such as stock index futures contracts are settled in cash.

**Delta**- A measure of how much an option premium changes given a unit change in the underlying futures contract. (Delta is often interpreted as the probability that the option will be in-the-money by expiration.)

**Exercise**- The action taken by the holder of a call option if he wishes to purchase the underlying futures contract or by the holder of a put option if he wishes to sell the underlying futures contract.

**Expiration Date**- Options on futures contracts typically expire on a specific date during the month preceding the futures contract delivery date. For example, an option on a March futures contract usually expires in February but is referred to as a March option because its exercise would result in a March futures contract position.

**Extrinsic Value**- The sum of the premium value of an option minus any intrinsic value. Out-of-the-money options are made up entirely of extrinsic value.

**Financial Instrument**- There are two basic types of financial instruments. There is a debt instrument, which is a loan to pay back funds with interest or an equity instrument that is a share of stock in a company.

**First Notice Day-** The first day on which a notice of interest to deliver a commodity in fulfillment of a given month's futures contract can be made by the clearinghouse to a buyer. The clearinghouse also informs the sellers who they have been matched up with.

**Fundamental Analysis-** A method of anticipating future price movement using supply and demand information.

**Futures Contract-** This is a legally binding agreement made on the trading floor of a futures exchange to buy or sell a commodity or financial instrument sometime in the future. These are standardized according to the quality, quantity, and delivery time and delivery location for each commodity. The only variable is price and this is discovered on the exchange trading floor.

**GLOBEX-** A global after-hours electronic trading system created by the Chicago Mercantile Exchange.

**GMO Grain-** GMO is an acronym for genetically modified organism. Generally used to describe grain that has been genetically modified to produce characteristics such as resistance to drought as well as weed and pesticide control. Such grains are very prevalent in the United States but are discouraged or even banned by the European Union, Japan and others.

**Gross Domestic Product (GDP)**- The value of all final goods and services produced by an economy over a particular time period, typically one year.

**Hedger**- An individual or company owning or planning to own a cash commodity, corn, soybeans, wheat, U.S. Treasury Bonds, notes, bills etc. and concerned that the cost of the commodity may change before either buying or selling it in the cash market. A hedger achieves protection against changing cash prices by purchasing (selling) futures contracts of the same or similar commodity and later offsetting that position by selling (purchasing) futures contracts of the same quantity and type as the initial transaction.

**ICE**- Short for the Intercontinental Exchange which is an Atlanta-based electronic exchange.

**Implied Volatility**- The forward looking theoretical value of the volatility of the underlying futures contract as it relates to the increase or decrease in an option's premium caused by the increase or decrease in the underlying futures contract's changes in volatility

**In-the-money-option-** An option having intrinsic value.

**Initial Margin-** The amount a futures market participant must deposit into his margin account at the time he places an order to buy or sell a futures contract or short an option.

**Intrinsic Value-** The amount an option is in-the-money.

**Introducing Broker-** A person or organization that solicits or accepts orders to buy or sell futures contracts and options on futures contracts but does not accept money or other assets to support such orders.

**Lagging Indicators-** Market indicators showing the general direction of the economy and confirming or denying the trend implied by the leading indicators.

**Last Trading Day-** This is the last day that trading may occur in a given futures or options contract month. Futures contracts outstanding at the end of the last trading day must be settled by the delivery of the underlying commodity.

**Leading Indicators**- Market indicators that signal the state of the economy for the coming months. Some of the leading indicators include: average manufacturing work week, initial claims for unemployment insurance, orders for consumer goods and material, percentage of companies reporting slower deliveries, and change in manufacturers' unfilled orders for durable goods, plant and equipment orders, new building permits, index of consumer expectations, change in material prices, prices of stocks, change in money supply.

**Liquid**- A characteristic of a commodity market with enough units outstanding to allow large transactions without a substantial change in price.

**Long**- One who has bought futures contracts, options contracts or owns a cash commodity.

**Margin**- There are many financial safeguards that have been implemented to ensure that clearing members perform on their customers' open futures and options contracts. Clearing margins are distinct from customer margins in that individual buyers and sellers of futures and options are required to deposit with brokers. Margins are determined by market risk and contract value.

**Margin Call**- A call from a clearinghouse to a clearing member or from a brokerage firm to its customer to bring margin deposits up to a minimum level.

**Market Order**- An order to buy or sell a futures or options contract of a given delivery month to be filled at the best possible price and as soon as possible.

**National Futures Association (NFA)**- The NFA is the industry wide, self-regulatory association for the United States futures industry.

**OPEC**- Organization of Petroleum Exporting Countries emerged as the major petroleum pricing power in 1973, when the ownership of oil production in the Middle East transferred from the operating companies to the governments of the producing countries or to their national oil companies. Members are: Algeria, Indonesia, Iran, Iraq, Kuwait, Libya, Nigeria, Qatar, Saudi Arabia, the United Arabs Emirates and Venezuela.

**Open Interest**- The total number of futures and options contracts of a given commodity that have not yet been offset by an opposite futures or options transaction.

**Option-** A contract that conveys the right but not the obligation to buy or sell a particular item at a certain price for a limited time.

**Option Premium-** The sum of money that the option buyer pays and the option seller collects for the rights granted by the option.

**Out-of-the-money option-** An option with no intrinsic value.

**Position Trader-** An approach to trading in which the trader holds onto a position for an extended period of time.

**Put Option-** An option that gives the purchaser the right but not the obligation to sell the underlying futures contract at the strike price on or before expiration.

**Seasonal Analysis-** Anticipating future price movements using historical price advances and declines of certain commodities to find a time line as to when those moves are most likely to occur during the year.

**Serial Month**- A short term option on a futures contract in which the underlying expires in a forward month.

**Spreading**- The simultaneous buying and selling of two related markets in the expectation that a profit will be made when the price difference between the two markets either widens or narrows. Examples include: selling one futures contract and buying another futures contract of the same commodity but with different delivery months: buying and selling the same delivery month of the same commodity on different futures exchanges; buying a given delivery month of one futures market and selling the same delivery month of a different but related futures market.

**Stop Order**- This is an order to buy or sell when the market reaches a specified point. A stop order to buy becomes a market order when the underlying futures contract is at or above the strike price. A stop order to sell becomes a market order when the underlying futures contract is at or below the strike price.

**Strike Price**- The price at which the futures contract underlying a call or put option can be purchased (if a call) or sold (if a put).

**Technical Analysis**- Anticipating future price movements using historical prices, trading volume, open interest and other trading data to study price patterns.

**Tick**- The smallest allowable increment of price movement for a contract.

**Time Decay**- The ratio of the change in an option's premium to the decrease in time until expiration.

**Volatility**- A measurement of the rate of change in price over a given period. It is often expressed as a percentage and computed as the annualized standard deviation of the percentage change in daily price.

**Volume**- The number of purchases or sales of commodity futures or options contracts for one trading day.

**Yield Curve**- A chart in which the yield level is plotted on the vertical axis and the term to maturity of debt instruments of similar creditworthiness is plotted on the horizontal axis. The yield curve is positive when long-term rates are higher than short-term rates; however the yield curve is negative when the long-term rates are lower than short-term rates.

**NOTES**

**NOTES**

# CONTRACT SPECIFICATIONS

**Currencies**

CME Group Euro FX Currency contract size = 125,000 Euros

Contract Months- March, June, September, December, Serial and Weekly

Minimum Fluctuation .0001 = $12.50

CME Group Japanese Yen contract size = 12,500,000 Yen

Contract Months- March, June, September, December, Serial and Weekly

Minimum Fluctuation .000001 = $12.50

**Financials**

CME Group Treasury Bond contract size = $100,000

Contract Months- March, June, September, December and Serial

Minimum Fluctuation 1/64 = $15.626

**Indices & Stocks**

CME Group S&P 500 E mini contract size = $50 multiplied by the index

Contract Months- March, June, September, December and Serial

Minimum Fluctuation .25 = $12.50


**Energies**

CME Group WTI Crude Oil contract size = 1,000 barrels

Contract Months- All

Minimum Fluctuation .01 = $10


CME Group Natural Gas, Henry Hub contract size = 10,000 mmBtu

Contract Months- All

Minimum Fluctuation .001 = $10


CME Group RBOB Unleaded Gas contract size = 42,000 gallons

Contract Months- All

Minimum Fluctuation .001/gallon = $4.20

CME Group ULSD Heating Oil contract size = 42,000 gallons

Contact Months- All

Minimum Fluctuation .001/gallon = $4.20

**Grains**

CME Group Corn, Soybeans and Wheat contract size = 5,000 bushels

Contract Months- March, May, July, September, December, Serial and Weekly

Minimum Fluctuation ¼ cent = $12.50

**Meats**

CME Group Feeder Cattle contract size = 50,000 pounds

Contract Months- January, March, April, May, August, September, October and December

Minimum Fluctuation .025 c/lb = $12.50

CME Group Live Cattle contract size = 40,000 pounds

Contract Months- February, April, June, August, October, December and Serial

Minimum Fluctuation .025 c/lb = $10

CME Group Lean Hog contract size = 40,000 pounds
Contract Months- February, April, May, June, July, August, October and December
Minimum Fluctuation .025 c/lb = $10

**Metals**

CME Group Copper contract size = 25,000 pounds
Contract Months- All
Minimum Fluctuation .05 c/lb = $12.50

CME Group Gold contract size = 100 ounces
Contract Months- February, April, June, August, October, December and Serial
Minimum Fluctuation .10 = $10

CME Group Silver contract size = 5,000 ounces
Contract Months- February, March, May, July, September, December and Serial
Minimum Fluctuation .005 = $25

**Exotics**

ICE Cocoa contract size = 10 metric tons
Contract Months- March, May, July, September, December and Serial
Minimum Fluctuation $1 per metric ton = $10

ICE Coffee C contract size = 37,500 pounds

Contract Months- March, May, July, September, December and Serial

Minimum Fluctuation .05 c/lb = $18.75

ICE Cotton #2 contract size = 50,000 pounds

Contract Months- March, May, July, October, December and Serial

Minimum Fluctuation .01 c/lb = $5

ICE Sugar #11 World contract size = 112,000 pounds

Contract Months- March, May, July, October and Serial

Minimum Fluctuation .01 c/lb = $11.20

ICE Orange Juice FCOJ-A contract size = 15,000 pounds

Contract Months- January, March, May, July, September, November and Serial

Minimum Fluctuation .05 c/lb = $7.50

**NOTES**

**NOTES**

Futures and options investments carry significant risk of loss and are not suitable for some investors. Past performance is not indicative of future results. This information can be considered a solicitation to enter into a derivatives trade. Use only risk capital when investing in high risk investments like futures and options.

The content within this book is for informational purposes only. No guarantees are being made to its accuracy or completeness. Contract specifications change from time to time. Contact the exchanges to find up to date information.

## Closing Message

It is very difficult for individual self publishers like this author to find enough publicity for their books when competing with the huge publishing companies and their enormous advertising budgets. If you found this book to be beneficial to you it would be very much appreciated if you would help me promote it.

There are many different ways that you can help me promote this book such as:

- Recommending the book to your friends and family;
- Reviewing it on your blog;
- Posting a review on Amazon or other book related websites;
- Giving a link to the www.tkfutures.com website;
- Or talking about it on your social media page.

Thank you for your help.

28651638R00074

Made in the USA
Charleston, SC
17 April 2014